The Dogs That Chase
Bicycle Wheels

*For Roy, who thinks he has no strengths
but is my strength*

The Dogs That Chase Bicycle Wheels

Ilse Pedler

Winner of the
Mslexia Poetry Pamphlet
Competition, 2015

SEREN

Seren is the book imprint of
Poetry Wales Press Ltd.
57 Nolton Street, Bridgend, Wales, CF31 3AE

www.serenbooks.com
facebook.com/SerenBooks
twitter@SerenBooks

The right of Ilse Pedler to be identified as
the author of this work has been asserted in accordance
with the Copyright, Designs and Patents Act, 1988.

© Ilse Pedler 2016

ISBN: 978-1-78172-337-1

A CIP record for this title is available from the British Library.

The publisher acknowledges the financial assistance of the Welsh Books Council.

Cover design: Jelena Mone and Jamie Hill

Printed in Bembo by Berforts Ltd, Hastings.

Contents

The Complete Science

We approached cautiously, the dogs in their crucifixion poses,
formalin-heavy air stopping up our nostrils, our throats,
forcing tears for the splayed exhibits in front of us that grinned
and looked the other way.

We discovered that muscles had bellies and heads, and cords
of arteries wove between them accompanied by nerves, flat as ribbons.
We were taught that everything had an origin and insertion and that the path
between rarely varied.

The anatomists in their white coats resected and peeled,
filleting their way out of our clumsy dead ends, calling us over
to marvel at the audacious inconsistencies, nodding when their
expectations were confirmed.

We repeated centuries in that high-ceilinged room, divided
muscles first seen in wounds on Galen's gladiators, tried to draw
with the accuracy of Vesalius and agreed with Harvey that life was more
than just ebb and flow.

So immersed were we in this delicate discovery of order,
we almost forgot our theatre would have a different audience.
We had no knowledge yet of the skin's elasticity,
its unexpected warmth.

Stumbling outside to be purified in the lighter air,
wrinkled latex fingers marked with the indentation of forceps,
I clung to Miller's dissection guide like my first alphabet,
where A was always for apple, B for ball.

Breaking the Code

Polydipsia, polyphagia
means too often.

We explored the sounds,
our tongues speculating
tentatively as we scribbled
down each new word,
not meeting each other's' eyes.

Tachycardia, tachypnoea
means too fast.

Some started dropping
the words into conversation,
I watched the ripples spreading
but waited until I could be sure
I could leave the surface like glass.

Dysuria, dyschezia
means too hard.

I had expected it to be easier.

Observations

We were assiduous pupils,
dissecting and describing like those before us,
chambers and humours, the glutinous bead of the lens,
but of flickers in peripheral vision and lives
lived in tension, we learned nothing.
Does the crow peck at the shine of the eye
mistaking it for a ripe currant
or knowing it releases the choicest juices?
Best we don't see.

We were governed by life cycles,
the neat dovetailing of hosts,
the satisfying logic of adaptation and vectors,
but no one told us that fleas seek out the blood of the newborn
and dying and fatten in black crusts around their eyes.
Does the Myxy rabbit find its way deliberately
to the side of the road, or does it stumble blindly
into the path of cars?
We look away.

Do you know that keds, sensing movement,
fly in straight lines from a dying bird to a new host
like black arrows?

Have you lifted decaying flesh
and seen a nest of maggots squirm back like sinners
from the light? I have,
I could teach you a little of what I know.

Blood Testing Piglets

Startled by our approach
they squeal and bounce off
with stiff rocking horse gaits,
then turn and peep out from under
unexpected eyelashes.

With a British Bulldog run
they dodge our hands then
bump and jostle together
at the other side,
all except the caught ones

who throw their heads back
in back-arching screams
at the indignity of being held.
Released, they scramble
and trip away but are soon

compelled forwards
with Mr Wolf steps
cold rubber noses
pressed against your leg,
a small hand slipped into yours.

Grunting Up★

Who would have thought that these great slab-sided beasts
who fall to their knees and slump belly up,
would sing this rhythmic, grunting lullaby?

Weight drops from back and loins but
swollen, undulating glands seem added on,
like a full frill at the bottom of a skirt.

The piglets rush to their particular nipple
and plug on, tongues curling, eyes closed,
chubby fingers, lined up, reaching.

And then she begins. This low throbbing,
this song to the milk flow,
this crooning hymn.

"Grunting up" the name given to the noise a sow makes when her
piglets are sucking.

The Importance of Air

Late afternoon when the low sun casts long
shadows on the field, the herd makes its way in order
to the collecting yard. The stockman slides the heavy
doors of the milking parlour open and then is gone
into the disinfected gloom. The first cow
shoulders her way in, eager to give up her milk

from her vulgar blue-veined udder. Dribbles of milk
are lost unnoticed from those waiting and form long
meandering creeks on the shit-splashed concrete. Each cow
a collection of monumental bones in a predetermined order
covered over with stretched hide. All softness gone
into the swollen bag they haul around waiting for the heavy

snatch of the cluster, each sucking rubber sleeve heavy
on the teat. Each udder drained and the white froth of milk
measured and emptied into the bulk tank and once she's gone
another takes her place quickly from the long
queue outside the parlour, never varying the order.
The stockman checks the ear tags, each cow

a number and in the office, each number, a cow's
worth of statistics and a coloured pin on the heavy
circular chart on the office wall. Every colour an order;
red for service, blue for calving, green to dry off the milk.
She shifts restlessly about the calving pen, her long
wait almost over. The yard is empty, the others long gone

back up to the field, the gate closed and the stockman gone
to clean the parlour. Her belly tightens and the cow
feels the first pains, she's been waiting for this all day long.
She finds a corner in the calving pen and lays, her belly heavy
with pressing calf, and her udder filling with the first thick milk.
She bellows through the pain, she knows there is an order

to these things. The stockman stops and listens, orders
his dog to stay and joins her in the calving pen, gone
is any thought of home. At last comes the gush of bloody fluid and milk
and the gasping rush of calf, huge and seal-like in its sac. The cow
licks with her long sure tongue and the calf lifts its head, heavy
with the importance of air. The cow breathes in calf all night long.

In the morning, the stockman gives the order to hold the cow
and before she can turn, the calf is gone. Her udder swells, heavy
with milk but he'll be back to take her to the parlour before long.

The Slaughterman's Dream

I dreamed that the line was reversed.
Through the rolling wall of steam
the split carcases loomed towards me.
The knives offered up their keenness
and the saws whined their defence.
Four hundred cattle.
Jerking and twitching on their knees
swollen tongues begging the lost air.
Their blood sucked back through screaming gashes
falling upwards to the clang of the gate
bolt jolting arm to socket.
And their huge brown eyes
staring into mine,
one by one by one by one.

Trapped

A path leads me to a tangle of buckled poles
and a Roe deer trawled in, trying to flip his fate,
kicking and twisting against the snare of cords
churning the grass around him in fury.

I cling to the loose lines like a kite in a gale
and exhausted he stops, mouth gaping,
bubbles of saliva around his blue slug tongue,
each sucked breath ending in a grunt.

His fish eye, dilated, looks through mine.
The sheet I slip over his head stills
the trembling to tautness. All muscles,
elastic stretched to the point of anticipation.

I sever each straining cord. They whip away,
cut after cut, and the only things in our world
are the cords and the knife and our breath
held somewhere high up in our throats.

In the Balance

We walked in silence that day
to Ladram Bay. Tired of fighting
we threaded our way through the gorse
at the cliff edge, determined to admire
the rusty sandstone spires.

Then we saw it. A kestrel balancing
on the back of the sea breeze.
A lightness of air infused bone, held.
Only the ruffle of wing tip feathers
revealing the difference between bird and sky.

We found ourselves standing closer
together, mouths open, staring.
It looks so effortless.
It must be such hard work
we said, almost at the same time.

Wearing Gold

My mother's wedding ring tightened
its grip on her plump finger year after year
until I thought it might disappear
into the cushions of pink flesh.
Sometimes, when I sat beside her I'd twist
it to see if I could release her.
You won't shift that, she'd say
If I end up in hospital they'll have to cut it off.
For years, I thought she meant her finger.

When we visited the Aunts I sat at their feet
fascinated by identical constrictions.
Rows of sausage fingers curled around cups of tea
or clasped under ample bosoms.
Some of the Aunts had two or even three bands,
narrow things that looked like they might snap.
When I asked why they were so thin, the eldest Aunt said,
they were big once, just like our men, but we wore 'em out!
Gold teeth flashed in the gales of laughter.

Years later, out with the girls and wedding rings
of our own, in between dramas of working
late and kids that wouldn't sleep,
we'd sort out the world
with a glass or two
of Pinot Grigio,
It was then I noticed
it wasn't only our bands
but our fingers that had worn thinner,
for some of us, our rings were so loose they fell off.

Following the Motorways

There were always maps.
Dog-eared rows on the bookcase,
framed prints on the wall,
and the weighty red atlas
by the side of the armchair,
each night a different country.

You would sit for hours studying
A roads and mountain ranges;
you welcomed the new motorways,
straight blue lines
leading in one direction only,
National Service, university, work.

Time was neatly divided:
climbing holidays in the Alps,
a season ticket to the Hallé,
politics and beer
in the back room of The George,
and your girlfriend.

It caught you out,
the sixth-month pregnancy,
no road through that one.
So you did the honourable thing,
then changed jobs, moved to a small town
in the Midlands, just off the M5.

I remember you in the evenings
your thumb fitting perfectly
in the worn spot on the atlas cover,
retracing old routes
trying to fix the shifting borders.

Play Zoo

First the railings have to be snapped together,
tight clips, tricky for little fingers
but that was the rule.

Next the lion house because the lion was the most
important. You could tell because his mouth
was open in a permanent roar.

The giraffe enclosure was the biggest, with lots of tall
trees for the giraffes to play with as they
plaited their necks together.

Finally, when everything was set up, the last task
was to put the lioness in with the lion
that's when the play really began

and the zookeeper in his peaked cap could go round
with his bucket distributing bleeding
chunks of raw meat.

Below the Bikini Line

Careful surgeons use the smallest needles. Other techniques include incisions below the bikini line; I didn't tell him I hadn't worn a bikini for years. Concealment is everything. One summer my mother took me to her hairdressers, she told me that I was old enough and that it was a special day. The hairdresser cut off my plaits. I remember the heat and smell of rotten eggs and the gossiping women netted and clamped under steel helmets cooing over my cheekbones. My father was silent when we got home. I grew my hair when I was pregnant; when I left hospital they told me I had stitches that would dissolve. If anyone asked, I told them it was worth it. The second time around a different hospital and I couldn't drive for six weeks, I told my mother I'd hurt my back, she didn't offer an opinion. These days, you can only see the scars in a certain light.

Suturing Secrets

We are divided into compartments,
separated by taut membranes,

glistening planes of connective tissue,
resilient boundaries.

Today this is damaged,
anaesthetized, surgically explored

your diaphragm is a torn curtain hanging
and like a peep show I'm drawn to look behind.

In the absence of pressure lungs hesitate
to inflate, do their best to conceal

the frantic convulsions at your core,
the struggle for rebirth every second.

I look perhaps longer than I should
at the shuddering flesh, the labouring

beauty, then I pull the curtain back over
and suture the secret inside.

Visit to the Vets

I'm listening when I say *how are you today?*
I'm listening when I tilt my head just so.
I'm listening when I say hello to Fluffy, Sooty or Rex.
I'm listening when Rex pees up the door.
I'm listening when you get a text and text back.
I'm listening when you let your kids climb on the table.
I'm listening when you answer your phone say, *I'm in the vets, can't talk,*
I'm listening when you carry on talking.
I'm listening when you say *I can't put my finger on what's wrong.*
I'm listening when you say *but I know he's just not right.*
I'm listening when you say you've looked it up on the internet.
I'm listening when you say, *are you sure?*
I'm listening when you ask me to predict the future.
I'm listening when he growls and you say *don't worry he won't bite you.*
I'm listening when he tries to bite me.
I'm listening when you ask me what's wrong and I've already told you.
I'm listening when you start telling me about your other dog.
I'm listening when I've heard the same thing five times already.
I'm listening when I plug my ears with the stethoscope.
I'm listening when you say *your job must be so interesting.*
I'm listening when you say *you vets are all rip-off merchants.*
I'm listening when you snap at your partner.
I'm listening when your kids go quiet and hold hands.
I'm listening to the sound of your self-importance filling the room.
I'm listening as your opinions start polishing their firearms.
I'm listening to the emptiness of your wallet in the silence.
I'm listening as your dead husband stands behind you putting
his overcoat around your shoulders.

Hounds- Stigmergy

Shoal quick
Turning in folds, shaping a course, streaming
In ripples across fields, noses ravelling in the scent, mouths
Gulping out their ululations, a tan and white symmetric skein
Moving in the wind's eye, cross country, downstream
Earthbound, packed shoulder to shoulder in a
Rolling collective that independently
Gathers actions which, incredibly,
Yield this synchronicity.

Terrier

Still stand   rock face of bales.
Tail stiff   flag but no wind.
Teeth sharp   lips grin.
Rat dart   snap drop.
Nose twitch   stroke shrug.
Hole dark   scent bright
      follow
         follow
            follow

The dogs that chase bicycle wheels

stare out of windows,
checking the boundaries
   checking the boundaries.

They have territories to protect,
       circling
           from the backs of sofas
   to front doors,
        to kitchens,
whole worlds held in their flat eyes.

Postmen breach defences,
dropping offerings
to be bitten, ripped and pissed on.

Straining to a point always
just in front of their noses,
the click
   clicking of bicycle wheels
tricking them into the frenzy of a chase
for the white scut of a rabbit.

Unceasingly they scout crowded horizons
for what is not there,
  will never be there.

Final Drawings

i.m. P.K.

I don't want to go to your funeral.
I don't want my mail returned to sender
or to pick up the phone and remember
you're not there. I want to hear more playful
musings on gibbous moons and the sculptural
vision of Henry Moore and the splendour
of squinches and quoins and all the other
terms you've learnt in your architectural
journey. I want to shout "don't take him yet,"
just let that fine-tipped pencil draw more dreams
with lines that don't confine but let in light.
If loss is measured in the space we leave,
you'll draw for us a glorious vaulted, bright
windowed, unending room in which to grieve.

Acknowledgements

Acknowledgements are due to the editors of the following anthologies and magazines where some of the poems have been published. *Spokes* Otley Word Feast Anthology, *The North. 14 Magazine, Angle Journal of Poetry in English, Brittle Star* and *Poetry Salzburg Review.* The following poems were successful in competitions 'Grunting Up' was third in The Bank Street Writers competition 2010, 'Following the Motorways' was commended in the Ware Poets Society prize 2011 , 'Trapped' was shortlisted in the Rialto Nature prize 2012 and In The Balance was shortlisted in the Rialto Nature prize 2015